LAMP OF THE BODY

LAMP OF THE BODY

poems

Maggie Smith

RED HEN PRESS   LOS ANGELES

Lamp of the Body

Cover image and author photo by Lesley Louden
Book design by Michael Vukadinovich
Cover Design by Mark E. Cull

ISBN: 1-888996-88-9

Library of Congress Catalog Card Number: 2005920070

Published by Red Hen Press

The City of Los Angeles Cultural Affairs Department, California Arts Council, Los Angeles County Arts Commission and National Endowment for the Arts partially support Red Hen Press.

First Edition

ACKNOWLEDGEMENTS

Thanks to the editors of the following journals in which certain of these poems, some in earlier versions or with different titles, first appeared:

Alaska Quarterly Review: "The One About the Wolf"; *Beacon Street Review:* "Horoscope (1)" & "Delilah"; *Beloit Poetry Journal:* "Psalm (1)" & "Psalm (2)"; *Crab Orchard Review:* "Singular"; *Florida Review:* "Country Warnings" & "Trompe l'Oeil"; ForPoetry.com: "Dorothy Waking" & "Job"; *Gulf Coast:* "The Poem Speaks to Desperation" & "The Poem Speaks to Nothing"; *Indiana Review:* "Nearsighted"; *The Iowa Review:* "Button"; *Many Mountains Moving:* "Moses"; *Mid-American Review:* "The Wife of Lot"; *Passages North:* "Re-imagined Evening with D." & "The Taste of Bone"; *Phoebe:* "The Poem Speaks to Danger"; *Poetry Northwest:* "Doubting Thomas" & "Memoir, in Circles"; *Prairie Schooner:* "The Beginning"; *Roanoke Review:* "Cana"; *Swink:* "See No Evil"; *Two Rivers Review:* "Stella by Starlight"

My deepest thanks to Kathy Fagan, Andrew Hudgins, Fred Leebron, David Citino, Jeredith Merrin, Kathryn Rhett, and Robert Flanagan: for their wisdom, encouragement, and friendship. Thanks also to Katie Pierce, who helped nurse many of these poems to health. Thanks to Lesley Louden, true friend and brilliant photographer. Special thanks to my friends and family, in Ohio and beyond. And to JHB, more than thanks.

Contents

3: Lamp of the Body

For Dabel

And for my parents

And for Jason

1
SEE NO EVIL

What you fear
will not go away: it will take you into
yourself and bless you and keep you.
That's the world, and we all live there.
—William Stafford

BUTTON

It's the '50s. You wear your dark Levis
cuffed up six inches. You have a cowlick.

There is a birthday party you won't attend
after a bad haircut. Your mother says,

Button, it's not the end of the world.
But the weathervane says, Button,

the end is near. It says the sky's gone
yellow with twisters. Small white stars

are invisible all day, but you hear them
chatter like teeth. Button, they say, why

not play with the others? Look at them,
having a fine time. But you wish the devil

on the neighbors. You wish them nothing
to pin the tail on. You wish the children

snatched up in the funnel, paper punch
cups still in their hands. The devil won't

call you Button. He says if you must
be haunted, at least be unashamed.

Home Movie

Sunlight seeping into the playroom.
The tiny kitchen set. Whole
plastic strawberries and dollops

of plastic cream on plastic cakes.
Three of us, each a color: blue,
yellow, pink. The shadow

of our dead black dog. Our father,
home from the taxidermist, enters
the frame, hangs the smallmouth

bass on the wood-paneled wall. Cut
to the yard: Yellow buries her toes
in the sandbox. Blue and I file

in and out of the play teepee.
A snake slips over my pink shoe
and into a hole by the buckeye tree.

When I run inside, shaken,
someone follows to capture me.
I am riding the horse on springs.

I rock until its hard nose grazes
the carpet, my own reflection tiny
and trembling in the camera's glass eye.

The Poem Speaks to Memory

If this is a hymn, I'm not
the one to sing it. I admit it:

Sometimes I think of your heart
as fleshy, diluted fruit. Watery

as a tomato, half-rotten,
begging salt. It's infuriating

how things seem to find their
way to your fingertips while

I have to wrestle anything
I can grab to the ground.

You are the bald light bulb
swinging over the past,

alternating harsh, soft, harsh
over the surfaces of its face,

a chiaroscuro. Look at you,
pointing to the sky, calling it

blue. Close your eyes, you say.
And it's still there, still blue

because it comes to you
that way, and you hold it.

If this is a hymn, I'll sing it
for questions neither of us

can answer, not for certain.
Tonight the crickets thick

around this house overlap,
repeating like a loop of song.

The shrill pitch trembles,
a kind of vibrato. Night grass

is a color for which there is
no name. Green and plum

come to mind, but the shade
does not exist. The color,

unnameable, glows when
it thinks no one is looking,

not even you. No one
rows to the island of his

childhood without rowing
through you, and you are

the deepest water there is.

HOROSCOPE (1)

Your dream: the word forming,
then a woman unbuttoning
herself from a white blouse.

Don't ask how I know this,
Aquarius, who the woman is,
or why the word lacked context,

as though projected onto a screen
in space. Had it been written
on a chalkboard, for example,

you may have leafed through
your dream dictionary for *chalkboard*
(see *blackboard*), all the while

missing the point: the word itself,
breasts so pale they appeared
to be lit from within. Aquarius,

there was something I meant
to write down today, didn't, and now
it is lost. But as the moon leaves

your house of knowledge
for that of doubt, self-loathing,
panic, I think of you waking,

feeling you should know
something you don't. The word is
forming in you. I can almost touch it.

PSALM (1)

Watch as the girls press
Father's shirts, snapping
each sleeve taut, creasing it

the way he likes. Forgive
the fabric. The girls do
what they can to smooth

and straighten, hissing
the iron's steam. Forgive
the house for its mirrors,

its dark wood that begs
another dusting. Forgive
the mat that welcomes.

It knows not what it does.
Forgive the greedy house
for wanting to keep

those who do its work.
At the end of the day,
lying in bed, they find

faces in the mottled ceiling:
an old man winking, one
shriveled ear cocked

toward them. Forgive
the man who watches.
Forgive Father for wanting

to keep the girls. And bless
the girls for doing his work,
pulling clean shirt after clean

MOSES

Leaving him with little more
than prayers that the pitch
would hold, his mother

hoped another would take him
from the river into her slender,
sunned arms, and name him.

Where will I be when you
open your drowsy mouth
to another's breasts as soft

as fresh figs, as though your
first breath is of her skin?
Far off as myth, lamenting

locks of your hair the birds
refuse to bring me out of loyalty
to her? What will I call you then?

Not love, but a memory
of loving. What a quiet
concession: a mother calling

her son by the name
another had chosen, *Moses*,
meaning *drawn from the water*.

FIRST SPRING

Delaware, Ohio

The Olentangy is the closest I come
to knowing a river. Its choppy water
bubbles like spit, breaks

around birch limbs, the rounded
ruins of a limestone wall.
Passing through the scent

of chives and lilacs, I see nothing
but leaves and dappled cows
nosing the slender grasses.

I imagine stealing corn
from the fields, pulling the pale
blonde strands from its pearly buttons.

As a child, I broke buckeyes
open with rocks and peeled back
the shells, rich and brown

as polished wood. I imagined
their poison meat would taste
as I thought marrow

would taste, mealy, and bitter
as human bone. Now this place,
with its spare, violent beauty,

breaks me open. I resign to spring
and its trappings: dark, bloodied
scraps of fur in the shoulders

of Bean Oller Road. Stones
begging to be turned. Everywhere,
the scent of lilacs and no sign of them.

Country Warnings

Child, any question worth asking
the sky can't be answered, so don't ask.

Instead, cheater that you are,
you look for answers in the form
of omens. If you speak to the sky

this way, you think it will show you
its secrets. Dead sparrow in the grass:

mercy will be asked of you.
Same bird, limp in a cat's mouth:
you will be betrayed. Mind yourself,

child. No one cares for a sinner
proud of her sin. When you go,

shut a black ace in the door
to ward off rain. Stay within
earshot. Anywhere past

the sound of my voice is too far.
Keep away from snake dens

near the creek, or risk a bite
in your heel like the Maynard boy,
two holes black as your eyes.

Don't look at me like that.
The sky hears what you pretend

not to ask. It's not above
sending omens of contrary.
If you think that feathers mean

a windfall, the sky will float some
into your hands without following

See No Evil

Fitting, how I am the one covering
my eyes in the photograph. Another
covers her ears, another her mouth.

This is years ago. My hair is dyed
an auburn so dark, it is nearly
violet. Hear No Evil is still

a schoolgirl, her neat bangs cut
straight across. Speak No Evil
is alive, her cigarette burning

down in the ashtray. Not yet
put to sleep, our black dog circles
before lying down, lapping cords

of smoke from the air. We hardly
notice as evil, a dark leak of it,
slips past the gates of our fingers

and into our bodies. Smoothing
the snapshot back into the album,
I forgive us for believing our small

hands were enough. I take mine
from my eyes. Another uncovers
her delicate ears and listens. The last

is speechless, as the dead are.

THE POEM SPEAKS TO DANGER

> *Beautiful things fill every vacancy.*
> —C.D. Wright

I am a buzzard sky, late
fall, the smell of kerosene.

The flicker of a deer's white
tail in the tree bones.

I am grass rusting.
In the lake, you are a fist

around a ponytail, the hum
of nearly stopped breathing.

A plane wrinkling a sheet
of night air. The belief

that everything ripe,
everything that will ever

ripen, has been picked.
Impossible. I am the mouth

that can hold more. I am
the moon watching the girls

swim, the night sky pucker
in the jet's pull. Softening,

flushed, I am a cheek.
Peachskin. The globe

of some new, ready fruit.

Dorothy Waking

I dreamt that we were back in Ohio.
Proving how little dreams know,
I asked about your kid brother,

picturing him as a boy, forgetting
he'd been found a few summers back
hanging from a tree at Alum Creek.

When I asked, a thunderhead
of black birds dropped like a tarp
on the long pines, plucked us up,

and carried us to that lonely country
where there are no fields of flowers,
no one dusting them with snow

as fine as confectioner's sugar.
Where there are no balloons
to carry us back to the lives we left,

and no white handkerchiefs to swish
bon voyage at the headstones, rows
of baby teeth growing smaller

below us, then vanishing.
In that country, the forest is all
shadow-trees, but the one where

your brother swings, where he swings
even now because time stopped,
is white and gnarled, a deer antler,

its bark like bone. His eyes are
missing, sockets dark as plum pits.
His brown hair scuffs in the wind.

Who can wake from that?
There is no telling what that wind
might blow home with us: crow

feathers, scraps of blue gingham,
black walnuts in green casings.
Their dark ink stains our hands;

even burning lye can't wash it off.
Who can wake from that? But we do.
We wake and point to others

in the room. *And you were there,
and you were there. And you.*

The Wife of Lot

The familiar burned bald, there was nothing
but the voice of God, tinny as a radio

through the clearing smoke, asking, tongue
in cheek, *Is this the proof you needed?*

Referring to me, stiff as a deer lick,
a pillar on which one might have inscribed

Seeing is believing. If just for an instant,
the fire at our backs shimmered on my face.

I turned out of human longing. More than
my love for you: my desire to witness.

Trompe l'Oeil

Once, while a man sped me down
    a back road in a gray pickup,
        I memorized my younger face

in the passenger side mirror,
    burned the opal at my throat
        and the white secondhand blouse—

tiny lilacs, puckered sleeves—
    into the undersides of my eyelids.
        My hair streamed

the color of hay out the window.
    Lettering on the mirror told me
        that despite how close

I appeared, I may have been closer.
    Something lit the opal's pink fires
        nearer the surface than I knew.

Things were not what they seemed.
    There was nothing I could reach
        out and touch. We parked

in a cloud of gravel dust. I hurled rocks
    into the quarry's dark mouth,
        bible black, and lied

about hearing them hit bottom.
    Inside every stillness, I believed
        something moved.

2
CHARLESTON GREEN

Hope makes a good breakfast
but a bad supper.
—Francis Bacon

RE-IMAGINED EVENING WITH D.

Raising the dead,
this is the way things happen:
rabbit, sleeve.

This time, I say
wake up, and she does.
She sits up on the gurney,

puts on her terry
scuffs and pink
windbreaker, and plucks

a cigarette, like a coin,
from behind my ear.
Once before,

I kissed her cold face
at the hairline, breathed
perfume I don't recall her

wearing, and waited:
nothing. As if to prove
nothing works

without instructions.
This time, I tell her
to wake up, and when

I offer her a light,
she does. She cups
her hand around the match

flare and leans in,
a bit of the old smoke
and mirrors.

The Taste of Bone

To this day I blame the high timothy
grass that rose beside Smothers road.

When the doe broke across my car
like a wave of wood, I took both

hands from the wheel and covered
my face. Later I thought, *of course.*

I live my life in fear, still chewing
her hooves in my sleep now and then.

Blood in my mouth and the taste
of bone. When I returned to the edge

of the field to reconcile my body
with hers, to breathe the frosted edge

off the keen air, I saw myself in her
landscape: the pear trees' hard red buds

fell, invariably closed. Frost, soft
to the touch, is lost upon touching.

Hay's faint sweetness dissolves
in the air. Years ago she fed me

her blonde bones, bland as chalk.
Even now, the taste on my breath.

Gone Missing

We were last seen on foot
    in St. Paul, Brainerd, Eau Claire.
        Our prints trailed off

from bars and filled with new snow
    or were never made. Somewhere
        we wait. Our gray

mouths gape, stopped in time
    and heaped with feathers of ice.
        Sifting through

the impossibly white dunes,
    a deputy may or may not
        discover, half-

obscured by the frozen skin
    of the river, one blue sneaker;
        32-waist jeans, the belt

unbuckled. Or no one searches.
    The air is so cold, it hardens
        to a sheet. Still,

our frozen skin may shine through
    delicate ice: a blue scroll
        tattoo on the small

of a back. Bones glow in the cold.
    A lace of frost spins itself
        on our secret faces.

Delilah

In the dream I wore my hair long and red
and boarded a train for your memory
of Poland. I rolled through violet clouds

of coal smoke to Warsaw, where she waited
out the rain with you. She fed the wood stove,
warming the narrow room you shared. The past

was just as I'd imagined: tenderness
down to the dove-colored walls; sheets of rain
slid over you, whole as touch. Tenderness

even as she stood above you, buried
her hands deep in your damp curls, and cut them,
handful after soft handful. Does it mean

less that I dreamed myself there? Finally
I could leave the color of doves and cold,
broad-sheeted rain behind. I could leave her

in Poland and return to you wholly,
forgiving her for strength you lost, your dark
hair falling audibly because it hurt.

The Poem Speaks to Doubt

You are what tells a woman
when she leaves a room

that the furniture disappears
behind her, the door, the room,

the entire building. The street
curls up behind each step.

You are what tells me
that I'm easily forgotten,

a shadow. On your dark
silhouette that passes

for a body, I am the jacket
you wear most of the time.

I give you shape, presence.
I speak for you in a clearer

voice than you deserve.
We have a few small things

in common, both curious
about our makers, both

pervasive. But you are formless
matter I shape into objects

of desire, currency I cash
for change. Again and again

I am sent like a canary
into the coal black of you.

I survive. A hologram, I rise,
edged: high definition, high

SELF PORTRAIT: THREE CANVASES

1

For every picture we were too ashamed to take, there is
something already half-lost: Paris, its three days of rain, its
voice I couldn't clear from my throat. Even the babies knew
more of the language than I did: subtract "b" from beef and
you have an egg. Walking back from the market, baguette in
my hand, was something from a film not as much about plot
as character.

2

Not as much about character as setting. Our postcard of a ve-
randa. My performance in those scenes was less than natural.
In Marseille we had almost reached our car when the train
doors began to slide shut. A fog welled up around our knees.
We were on the platform when France pulled away, no hand-
kerchiefs to wave at her.

3

We came thinking this place would be lit by us. It was not.
On the map, the boundaries between places were made
of smoke that kept drifting, burning our eyes. Who would
believe we were so close to Africa, Switzerland, Spain? Bells
rang on the hour, slightly muffled by the cold. What we do
not remember, we invent.

The Fever

Your mother's blue robe
recedes into rooms lit by

televisions, rooms wavering
blue as aquariums minus

the fish. In the darkness
of your childhood bedroom,

the vaporizer billows steam
the scent of throat drops.

Stranded in fever, you ask her
to crack the door and leave

the hall light on. Downstairs,
beyond the wooden banister

with its spindles, the television
bathes her in light and flickering

applause. Your mother whirs
like an engine in the mint air.

Her robe is impossible to see
against the night, that enclosure.

Who could distinguish her, a blue
painting, from her blue frame?

DOUBTING THOMAS

I was tired of the smoke
and mirrors. The loaves, the fish,
but not nearly enough time.

What could I say to him, friend
I buried, when he woke and called to me
softly from the shadows?

Go now. The business of faith
bores me. I could take it or leave it.
Understand, I touched his wounds

because I wanted to feel
his warmth on my own hands.
If I doubted anything then,

it was humanity. Disillusionment
is what happens when men
dabble in magic. Celebrity is a tree

on fire and of the thousands
standing near, none is near enough
to lick the flames from your face.

Once the embers burning
above us were enough. I believe
he doubled back from death

to breathe home's balmy air,
to stand in light among us
one last time beneath the high

heavens. For this brotherhood
I lose a brother; I spit upon the lot
we've drawn. So much for twilight

spent floating on the river, talking
of women we were not to love,
and of their skin scrubbed sweet

as tangerines. So much for nights
we passed in the desert, drunk
under the young stars whose names

were new. Once my friend
agreed: No one could recognize
each luminous body across

this broadening, eternal cleft.

The One About the Wolf

Dead, you don't forget my name, my face.
You never wander off. You don't mistake
another's house for yours. You never sleep.

Dead, your tuck-in's done. You never tell
the one about the girl's red hood. You never
snore yourself awake, forget to leave

the door ajar, and I believe the wolf
is just your breathing. Dead, you never cook
your cabbage soup. Or shoo me from your glass

of *hozzem blozzem*—bourbon, water, ice.
You never haunt. Or hear me ring the bell.
I wait, but no one answers. You're a truant.

An awful hostess. Dead, you never give
the one about the wolf disguised as child,
malignant as benign, a happy ending.

It tricked us. Swallowed you alive. Inside,
no muffled cries. It's just as well. The woodsman
can't use his bowie knife to cut you out.

You're dead. But now, you don't forget my name
or call me by my mother's. Dead, you never
speak to me. You never bare your teeth.

CHARLESTON GREEN

In the portrait of us against
white—only our faces, our eyes—
I painted our mouths on

upside-down and screaming.
The dark vowels left
invisible were ice-cold,

murky as a lake. What nipped
at our skin in that imagined
water was not grief

but worry, its teeth grown
soft with use. The portrait
wanted to be of our voices,

but I couldn't mix the shade.
No green-black was green
or black enough. Instead,

the space around our mouths
is blank. Upside-down,
we nearly smile. My eyeglasses

lay beside my paints
and brushes now, a still life.
Through them, nothing is seen.

JOB

Darkness plows its furrow here.
I am nothing now but a purse of bones.

Skin for skin, Satan said. *All that a man has
he will give for his life.* What was given me

has been taken away, my cup drained
to the dregs. Gone, seven sons

and three daughters, the sky spiraling
with their black hair. And for what?

To prove the worst can happen
at any moment, and always does.

Darkness digs a rut miles deep
somewhere in my field. It's as if

I wander blind, hardly trusting
my own steps not to lead me

down into it. Who here deserves
forgiveness? Who could possibly

bestow it? I asked for an apology,
but one was not owed me. Forgive me:

I have uttered what I did not understand.
Worse happens to better than I.

The Poem Speaks to Nothing

Unbuttoned, opened into
whiteness, you are so pure

it is grotesque. You lie
quietly, your breath so shallow

I can barely see your chest
rising, falling. Dumb as a pane

of glass, you let me see
clean through you. Rooted

deep in absence, you know
less than you think: names,

not faces. The math of you
is nonsense: only zeros

to carry. I multiply and
divide you. You look on,

bored, impotent. Rolling your
blind eyes, you refuse me.

You're all pins and needles,
crackling television snow

to sift through. But I shape
your hollows in my image,

one by one, and fill them
wholly. Reveling in coolness,

you beget yourself. I paint
my face on your blank canvas.

STELLA BY STARLIGHT

She's waiting for us inside. Someone's name is

on the tip of her tongue. She calls my cousin
the girl, and my cousin's son, *the baby.*

Today the girl brought the baby. Night comes on,
a blue wash, cadet blue. The rain is nearly

invisible. She's waiting inside, convinced
the sofa has been re-upholstered again

in what proves to be the same damask,
worn and blue, she's had thirty years.

Lucid moments are cruelest. She asks me
where I've been. And then she's gone,

calling her cigarette *knife,* grinding out
her *knife* in the pewter ashtray

shaped like a seashell. Her blue house
slippers are embroidered with pink roses,

green leaves. Her hair is set. Her heart is
an instrumental on the old radio. She hums

the melody. It's a song and the name is

3
Lamp of the Body

What does not die deserves to live.
—Donald Revell

The Beginning

In those days I was a door blown open
by wind. My body was strange to me:
What was I made of? It was a question
I was slapped for asking. I knew only
the field's sweet, dark soil smelled
good enough to eat. I peeled back the husks
until my hands were raw. Soon the soft,
edible fruits of the body were all I knew
of that place. I peeled to the skin and cradled
a grown man with my body, rolling
over him, over him, matting the cut corn.
There was light then and the light was good.

AUBADE, SAN FRANCISCO

What can you do when you know

life could not be simple again
without the novelty of simplicity.

Before leaving California, I opened
the hotel windows, half-expecting

Ohio air, the clean scent of apples
from the bay, wanting it crisper

and sweeter than it was. California,
I imagined, its whole magnolias

fallen and browning underfoot,
was so far gone. It was Peter Fonda

careening down Pacific Coast Highway
in a pale blue Karmann Ghia,

checking his teeth in the rear-view
when, suddenly, the mirror fills

with white-blossoming dogwoods,
the steady Midwestern landscape,

an entirely different green from this.
He wears off-white linen to a dinner party

and drinks too much chilled Riesling
on so-and-so's two-tiered veranda.

He eyes the bluffs and the twinkling
strands of traffic, sucks the last bit

of translucent meat from a shrimp,
and knows there's no going back,

things have taken their course.

There is a sense of touch
transcending the fundamental
distinction: here, there.

I am paraphrasing myself here.
There is no such thing
as an open circle. We curl in,

touching foreheads, creating
a closed circuit, inadvertently
falling asleep. His subsequent

dreamlessness, a sky cast over.
I am more out than the stars.
My view from the plane is that

of one traveling alone. Look
at the constellations now, noting
how the lines have changed

over time. We recall them
differently than they are.
Any point on the circumference

of a circle could be the beginning,
middle, end. Old English version:
this is *weird*. I don't want my life

back. My small thumb, the nail
chewed to the quick, is the same
as his but scaled down exactly one size.

Modern translation: this is *fate*.
Peas still in the pod. A green taste,
reminiscent of cool water.

Was it even my suitcase
I lived out of all week, folding
and unfolding? And where

do I expect to find myself in these
words kept at room temperature?
I unlearned the water from him

by floating on my back. Vertigo:
the sixth sense, we assume, if five
is still touch. He suspended me

on the warm green surface of the lake,
his right hand cupping my head, his left
at the base of my spine. My heart

was light in my chest, keeping me
afloat. A column of clouds, a banister
without stairs. Think light: a blue

freckled bird's egg. Think soft: stepping
out into the rain. His grandmother is dead.
Send the pale roses with the pretty

pink tips. Meaning: sympathy
is inaccurate. A name is not a name.
Helen-uh, never *Helay-nuh*.

We took our grief to the fireworks
and sprawled on the lawn with it
beneath weeping willows of golden ash.

It was Independence Day. From now
on. Until then I hadn't noticed.
There is a point where even the clouds

stop, exclaiming, *The sky, the limit!*
Distance that is mathematically
sound. My grandfather is dying.

Turn your head as you are floating
and put your ear to the water. Listen.
It sounds like a womb. The body

is your own. You either reconcile it
or it takes you, frame by frame.
Reconsider the night the sun left

without us. We stood in the grainy
darkness of the clearing, looking out
as if the ship we had meant to board

had set sail. There is no such thing
as an open circle. The airplane windows,
in my dream, went blank as sheets

of paper. Our books kept falling
open to the same scenes: a clear
lack of skyscrapers, a column of clouds.

Then I woke. From now on.
A green taste, reminiscent of cool water.
There is a sense of touch.

Nearsighted

> Child I have not had,
> I am your eyes.
> —Beckian Fritz Goldberg

I have not seen enough for you:
a cloud moustaching the moon.

Others shaped like circus animals—
a camel, a bear, a seal—spin
above you like a mobile.

The night's inkblot spreads
across your nursery ceiling.
The bell of a mother's face.

Before I turned nine, trees
were soft globes. Then each leaf
emerged on the other side

of my thick glasses. I wish
better eyes for you, but the same
blue, with yellow centers.

Child, I've seen for you only
what I can: nothing

precisely. My hands lift you
from sleep. My blurred face
floats above you, ringing.

Panes of wheat overlap
for rusted miles in this country.
With a trick distance performs

on the eye, suddenly they're one
sheet the color of singed hair,
the dog fur texture of harvested grain.

Even *forest* is singular standing in
for plural—a loose bundle of trees,
the white elbows of half-lit

birches multiplying. A cloak
of birds rises and falls in unison.
Chimney smoke, the gray spools

of hay blanched in the fields
are a pattern repeating, a printed
fabric on which the sloping

necks of horses become one
infinite curve. We crave what resists
duplication, the red fox racing

alongside the car. The one picket
standing in a field, the rest fallen,
carted away. The moon sharpening

its white edge against our eyes.

The Year's Last Bees

The rough fur of the year's last bees
prickles, sensing death. Hollows
of trees are thick with it, coarse

and swarming. Her cigarette
smolders. Jewelry chimes inside
a delicate veil of smoke. Someone

wheels her backwards through glass
doors into the garden, wearing
a path in the carpet. She imagines

red throats of flowers, tangles
of leaves, but frost beards the lawn.
Verging on numbness, breath

sharpening in her lungs,
those dusty jewels, she is alive.
Deep in her blouse, a gold pinecone

sings on its chain. A few things
try to live. In desperation, sting.

The Poem Speaks to Progress

You burn the path to the new
world, and for this world

I would be disassembled,
then rebuilt. In your name,

black pendulums of wrecking
balls swing into cinder block.

Sticks of dynamite wrap
support beams. I can't

get enough of glass ground
into your boot soles—

that splintering, crunching.
You scene-stealer, sometimes

I want to slam the door
when you come whirring

around, all bells and whistles.
I still grieve for what I was,

what I knew before.
What I didn't. They say

that the universe expands
so slowly, we can't possibly

feel it. But tonight feels
like a room rearranged, stars

hung on all the wrong walls.
You break in, rummage

through my rusted fixtures,
and steal nothing. But

Horoscope (2)

Libra, you're haunted by children.
You find their baby teeth
under your pillow, transparent

as kernels of sweet corn.
You leave dimes for small ones,
quarters for molars, hoping

they'll pocket the change
and leave you. Don't ask me why
they stick around, unwanted.

In reoccurring dreams they wait
on the front stoop with a year's
worth of unread newspapers,

shining penlights at the door
you refuse to open. Libra,
your ruling planet moves into

uncharted territory. Pony-tailed,
all cheeks, the small girls follow.
And the boys, their miniature

corduroys and oxford shirts
like dolls' clothes. You hear them
in their best school shoes,

using their inside voices.
Well-behaved or not, they startle
like an intrusion, a breach

of privacy. Believe me, Libra,
when I tell you their tiny lights
may yet pierce the keyhole.

PSALM (2)

Let the girls dance,
their white legs, bell
clappers in layers of skirts.

Let them play in the house
that holds secrets under
its tongue, dark lozenges.

Black smoke piping
from the chimney means
the swifts were not

swift enough. Father,
after lighting the fire, runs
outside to watch

the birds not escape.
But let them. Let the girls.
Who knows this song?

It is the East Coast. Apples
turn to wood. The girls,
shut in, roll them against

the closet walls. Perhaps
they should have minded.
They should have eaten

what was before them.
Slipped the hobby horse
back into its play stable.

Let the girls dance
despite their wrongs.
Let them find a way out.

Push on a bookcase
that revolves into a new
room. Let them steal

down the dark corridors.
Let their skirts ring
faintly in the light.

LAMP OF THE BODY

> *The eye is the lamp of the body. So, if your*
> *eye is sound, your whole body will be full*
> *of light.*
> —Matthew 6:22

Tonight you're sailing over the tiled roofs
in your blue pajamas, over our family's

streets—Redwood, Lilacwood, Liberty,
Hummingbird. I can see you by the light

of my own body. It fills me to the skin.
I can see your cigarette ash is growing

inches long, and you've forgotten it.
You're busy now, navigating the stars,

dewing each blade of grass with a fingertip.
Everywhere I see smoke dissolving, a soft

trick of the eye. The ash bends, then
drops off. From here I can see pink roses

on your blue house slippers. Come down.
Do you know my face? That's me waving

from the one lit window on a street
you don't know. I'm lighting it with my body.

CANA

For weeks the dreams called you
my husband. I hadn't the heart

to correct them. Besides, dreams
are often confused, anachronistic,

analog to nothing. One minute,
we're the way we are. The next,

as in the dream where you fell
shaking and sweating into diabetic

shock, everything goes to hell.
(When I tried to dial an ambulance,

the numbers all turned to nines
and ones.) If dreams are transmitted

from a place where we've already
happened and failed, then miracle,

another form of imagination,
has its limits. One minute: water,

the acceptance of impossibility.
The next: wine, the dreams all but

calling me *wife* or *widow,* the moon
soft and white as a wedding mint.

After Reading "Mock Orange"

Already, it was so:
the scent of orange blossoms
at the window, sun-jostled, bearing

the sting of the finite.
I thought of birds in those branches
as jewels, hard, refracting

light onto our walls, and knew
whatever gleaming they may have done
was not for us.

Knowledge came
disguised in sweetness
and with such ease, it astonished.

We knew, eventually, we would want
different things. Then
we started wanting them.

The Poem Speaks to Desperation

Your whole radio is dialed
gray with static. Before

the bell rings, I know it's you,
all nerves, your grip muscular

but trembling. You burn
inside the rifle's black throat.

You fuel the failed attempt,
the old Pontiac refusing to sail

nose-first into the reservoir.
I wait in the water, the cold,

stinking dark of it, willing
against you. Deep in your gut,

I light small fires for attention.
I inhabit you, a nest of bees

in your mouth. You cannot
swallow without waking them.

Inside you, my ribbons
of smoke rise into coded

letters. I have the last word.
On the tip of a tongue,

suddenly, I am what swarms.

BIOGRAPHICAL NOTE

Maggie Smith was born in 1977 in Columbus, Ohio. After receiving her M.F.A. from The Ohio State University, she taught creative writing on a one-year residency at Gettysburg College. Smith's poems have appeared in *The Iowa Review*, *Indiana Review*, *Florida Review*, *Prairie Schooner*, *Mid-American Review*, *Poetry Northwest*, *Swink*, *Crab Orchard Review*, *Gulf Coast*, *Alaska Quarterly Review*, *Connecticut Review*, *Phoebe*, *Beloit Poetry Journal*, *Passage North*, and other journals. Her chapbook *Nesting Dolls* won the 2004 Pudding House National Poetry Chapbook Competition. She has received two Academy of American Poets Prizes and an Individual Artist Fellowship from the Ohio Arts Council.

Printed in the USA
CPSIA information can be obtained
at www.ICGtesting.com
JSHW080007150824
68134JS00021B/2325

9 781888 996883